BLUES: *The Story Always Untold*

BLUES

The Story Always Untold

---

by Sterling D. Plumpp

Another
Chicago
Press
Chicago

Published by ACP, Box 11223, Chicago IL 60611

Cover Art, *Mother with Child, July 1939* by Bill Traylor
from the collection of Judy A. Saslow, © 1987 Judy A. Saslow.

Design by Raymond Machura

Grateful acknowledgement is given to the following publications
for permission to reprint the works listed: *River Styx*, "Mississippi
Griot." *Nommo: Twenty Years of Writing in Black Chicago*, "Official,"
"Big Maybelle," "Speech." *Triquarterly #73*, "Muddy Waters,"
"Robert Johnson," "Saturday Night Decades." *The Black Nation*,
"It Is the Blues," "Inherited Blues," "Billy Branch," "SOB,"
"Groove," "The Blues I See," "Burning Up in the Wind," "Blues
for Leon Forrest." *ACM*, "190," "197," "201," "216." Also the
author wishes to express his appreciation to Billy Branch for
seventeen years of friendship and his brilliance in continuing the
tradition; to Bill Ferris for his dedication to scholarship and
efforts that will insure that the blues will find their rightful
place; to Jerry Ward for endurance in reading many versions of
this manuscript while in formation; and to Amiri Baraka for his
support.

ISBN 0-9614644-8-8

LC # 88-71680

Distributed in the United States by
ILPA, Box 816, Oak Park IL 60303

For JEM, for being the enchanting whispers to touch me, move me away from the depths of my blues in these terrible times.

Preface

The organ swings
yesterday from Jimmy
Smith's cooking.
Blue notes filter
Burrell's judgment
from testimony of a
guitar. Freedom/I
say Martin and
Malcolm X. Live in
the beats. The sit
ins, ride drums way
down Blakely's armor of
connections. His wrists
calling names. I for
got in terror. Simply
the blues/reigns
from bases in im
provisations's, arms.
Some longing, some
missing, wanted
aspirations. Wait
in distant rooms of
my mind. And I long.

The best fruit in
my history's garden.
I reach/with feelings

Identity

I/the poor, shadows
are crying. Bowl of
blues at my hours.
Bowl of blues
lowdown blues
at my hours.
I/the poor, earth
parched by crimes.
Long rows of blues
mangled with boll weevils
of greed. Rows of blues
lowdown blues filling
up my seconds.
I/the poor, encyclopedic
scarecrows lining fences
of my distance, my journeying
way of improvisations.
I travel drought. My
father planted wells
in voices of history.
Rows of blues, them dirty
blues tangled in my weeks.
I/the poor, silence recording

ledgers of my generations.
I give you windows
in darkness, ears
in silence. I ritualize:

Mississippi Griot

(for Ann Abadie)

He sat there
on the porch of eternity
like a melon on a bed.
Emitting
dark seeds of prophecy
through teeth of storms.
Mississippi griot,
Mississippi son, native of
genocides, emitting
black seeds of prophecy.
He
had the river
inside him.
It was his tale and memory.
Wish I was a mocking bird
Out on a limb to swing.
They done stole all I own
and all I can do is sing.
He had the river in
side him.
Patted his feet and cat
fish fell from his muddy rhythms.
Crying

cause they woman done gone.
Crying
cause the blues from depths
upsetting their veins.
Mississippi griot,
Mississippi son.

He
bent strings and my grandfather's
fields were flooded and I
stood out
on a
red
clay hill/looking at
the pain.
I used to feel. The blues
he played built the levee
as the river with
in him ran down
through my eyes and my pen
trembled like Lucille does
when B.B.'s tender fingers
stroke her hair in tongues.
The
delta rolled out
beneath his shadow
and he sang shacks
along perimeters of debts.
The
crowd, stunned
ran to banks and
his muddy red words
moaned down stream.

He
had the river in
side him and sang it.
It
was his burdened story of time.
It
was his lush epic of ancestry.
It
was his personal chronicle of trials.
It
was his collective psalms of testifying.
It
was his blues.
He
sang for those
who done lived out the dues.

Ain't got nothing, yall,
just my empty broken hand.
Said I'm broke, yall,
All I got is a empty hand.
Would be a rich man
if I could blues you to understand.

He
takes Emmet Till's decomposing body
from the river in
side him. Lifts it
with the fork of his cries
to a corner
in my skull. And I
scream terrors of multitudes.

Every bone
from nameless black victims interred in the
river
recite their identities
in pulses breathing.

Mississippi griot
Mississippi son.

Water rises
to his waist. The river with
in him flows.

The crowd
watches history.
He laughs
the bewildering troubles away.
Calls un
known poets to rituals.
The river is my history.
I was born with
in the mud in
side his lyrics. Snakes,
turtles,, and frogs
were my play
mates in the river.
He
has it in
side him.
It
is my history and

it
is my autobiography
when he sings.

Inherited Blues

Every day/complaining:
Minding roots of noise.
I hear. I live. Mean
times howdying howdying
fingers; poking fun
at me/like mocking birds.
Every day/the sun rises
half-way, stops, sinks
back down. The anvil
of hard times/ in my chest.
Every day/reminding myself:
just how long/road I'm on.
Nothing but troubles/troubles
in my blood. Nothing/swing
with but skin and soul.
Travelling/nobody seeing me/
a sack over my head. Nobody
hearing/I am alone. I beat/
the anvil and moan. Beat/and
moan.

It Is the Blues

(For Bill and Susannah Ferris)

Cuckle burrs snarled
in my hair. And breezes
pesky as mosquitoes.
It is the blues/crawling
over evening for a
feast. Nobody hears
my dungeon screams
as loneliness tapdances
inside my skull.
The windmill of moans
churns and the long gulf
of pain stretches in veins.
It is the blues. The grassy
head of anxiety/coughing
up dues/ The under ache
drowning my name. The crackling
hurt sizzling in pots
of memories. Loss and troubles
boiling in my heart. It is
the blues/lowdown in evil.
Sending their spikes
through teeth and spines.
The upset stomach of dreams/

dizzy and longing for rest.
The big boss man of pleas/
calling from his knees.
Pleading for his woman/needing
cause she is gone. Crying
in the wind/begging comfort.
It is the blues. The long road/
crooked with yesterday's steps
and zigzagging with tomorrow's
trails. The wandering journey
through blistered feet. It
is the blues. The shouts
nobody claims to make. The groans
only hard to bake. The pleas
to a hawkish wind. Laughter
that'll make evil grin. Wide-mouthed
screamed out clues. A life paying
its dues. It is the blues. . .

Muddy Waters

(for Jerry Ward)

He
put a moving in my father.
I
saw it ripe as liver
hung
up
on hog
killing day.
And they made
the image they dreamed
from it.
I
saw gods in their strides,
feisty bold, desires tilted
like derby hats. As
they made
space. He
put a moving in my father.
I
saw him down
on his spirit/breathing
legends into brown eyes.
Jump

joy
roots of sudden power.
Mixed
tastes of green 'simmons
and garlic.

To suck groans from smiles.
As
they pocketed the meaning
in their genes and
kept evil out
side vows in their dance.
Turned
quietness to flames in loins.
Shocked
segregated fingers
to clenched fists.
As
men paraded.
They
left shadows of lynchings and
made images.
Hung
them above creation
to drip
on generations.

He
put a moving in my father

Depth

The story with
in the hole. With
in the story
with/in the
hole. Worrying
life of stars.
The story/quilted
by time: patched
and hid among rags,
pushed down. The
blues you can dig
dig
dig
deep with
in and find an
other tale. Music
saluting bones of
yesterday. Marrowed
by tongue/rhythms
lead to
confess about my
baby. Blues/a mud
pond I was born

in. The long ditch
my mother crawled
from adolescence.
The story with
in a hole: blues/
a memorial. Affirmation
from silence.
Celebration from
denial's mouth. I
was born from
my mother's callings
deep beneath the hole.
I was born in her
affirmation of
will and the
blues held claims
to my name

With
in the story
in the story.
I forgot the pain
I caused. Slept nights
crazy on winged moments
tiers of ecstasy.
You
belong to me to
night: one million
layers of unity
I give. I loves
to beg; don't ever
leave my blues. With
in the tale. Be

neath the hole. Please
blues, don't ever
say good
bye. My plea
is affirmation
in the turning point
          turning point
I reached. With
in the story: blues
I hold on. Can't
worry about tomorrow.
Been down since
the day I was born
in a hole. Big-legged
may carry me to
my grave. With
in the story in
the blues I got.
Blues
begins a language
I speak. Sustains
a music/which dances
in my veins.

Player

Lil' Bro
never under
stood the silences.
He
saw between dew
and wells gone
dry. The cakes
pies
roast
fruit
candy
and little
gifts
be
side the hearth.
He
took as duty.
As rights.
He
for
got the silence.
After
each feast

when cold
and empty
boxes
decorated the
front
room. At
thirteen
Momma said
she'd give
him a few
dollars.
He did
not feel surprise
drip
pin
g from his heart.
She had
told him
bout boys
who growed
up
too fast. Who
lost belief.
Said some
slept with
they eyes
open
and Santa Claus
chunked ashes
in them.
He
had doubted.
And when

his fourteenth
Christ
mas rolled a
round he
held the
few dollars
in his pockets.
There were no
candy
nuts
apples
or oranges.
When agitated
the fire
threw ashes in
to his face. As
he
attempted to coax
more heat.
His grand
father
lay dying
under quilts
and silence.
With
in him a blues
was prophesied
in his a
loness and he
failed to catch
it.

Wailing

The funerals you
didn't attend.
Say
something a
bout years.
About dreams. Some
where back
in 1955 a boy
inside a middle
aged man. Watches
a grand
father. Santa Claus
stopped coming
the year before.
He woke
up
to cold house.
Smoke gathering
space for its
baby.
The old man
in him shows
his face in the looking

glass and the
silence he hears
under covers
pulls sunshine
from his Christmas

Twenty
five years
later. He listens
to his mother;
wailing
a blues
she done got
over. Wailing
bulbs from trees
and wrappings
from packages.
Wailing
her obituary
on ticks
of a clock
in his dreams.
Next year
he counts
the stars
to see
if they all
there.
A grand
father is distant
in his face
and he wails
the hurt his dreams

see as last day
of the year sinks
in his memory.

B.B. King

The million dollars
he got in his voice
indebt my mother.
She
slops demons of coal oiled
nights her loneliness
and he
rises out of clods of needles
scrubbing wax for pleas.
The woman
in him cries sunsets
over promises. And I
a poor boy hears
the blues boy
I long in settlements of mosquito
inoculations at burnt ragged initiations.
His voice
climbs from maggots in dreams,
walks up muddy hills of stillness
and hangs a breeze
out over misery-soaked visions.
I was born in

side the woman in
side his falsetto-tarrying sound.

He plays
to give us time.
To give us rhythm.
To give us humanity.
To give us recognition.
To give us signature.
To give us music as doves.
He plays
sensuality in dust:
sagas rusted by denials.
He plays
selves into looking
glasses we dreaded.
At night
I hold out his voice against light
in windows of faith and
tomorrow trudges
through briars'
recalcitrant bitterness.
Encamped
in motions I long.

Deep Down

(For A Poet I Know)

An angel comes
in Lil Bro's blues,
sits on a couch, strips
down to her bones
and prays history. Hangs
her wings side
his perspiration, gets
down on his shadow, rolls
and tumbles out
her pleas. Gets buck
naked and calls the onion
scent of her savior's
overalls. Dresses in
Lil Bro's blues
and disappears inside
his rhythms.

Links Hall

Blues
now you done thrust
the umbilical hook
from my child
hooded crosses of
fears. Done hooked
that uncharted journey
into chaos.
I could
not live. That
song death clasps
in its silent palms.
I could
not sing.
Blues
you done gone
in my sleep
and unwound tortures
I invented in
my fountain of discord.
You pull me
in like a revivalist
reeling in his sheaves

of metamorphosis.
Blues
you done stripped me
down to baptismal
rituals. Immersed me
in hands right and
certain of courses
in the dreads. I
once could
not refine to language.
Blues
you done gone
taken my death:
the silence
and myth laying in open
communal regard. Some
where in Mississippi's
ornaments. Done hooked
me with afterbirth
of a million centuries.
My mother cried in songs
of pain and nommo/for my
arrival. Stripped me
down to initials
of diasporic pleas and
left me
changing.

Bessie Smith

Furrowed meanings.
Middlebustered origins of
speech. Took her in
sides, called epics of the
down and out multitudes.
Before a nation, a scattered
fragmented tribe of sufferers.
Their epic laden woes
crouched in her in
sides moaning like a drunk
boll weevil. She rises
from back
doors carved on memories
to loom history
round skeletons of lynched dreams.
Stands
way
up
on a limb of wind
her pig
feet
in one hand
and gin in

the other. Takes the flood
that washed a
way fields and houses
from her eyes.

Cries
into drought of souls.
Longing
their days.
Gives
identity to a language
blooming from a back
street nation.
Its history
bleeds from sound as
the citizens
come out to get
baptized in
side their pain.
She
calls the hurt to an open
wound in
side her and it siphons
their pain into epics
she is bellowing
over peaks of time. She
calls
diasporic exiles
to tenements in bosoms of her words.
Takes
her loneliness to
each
empty

bed, grooves springs
to joychains as beds
weep ecstasy.

I sing gossip no
body wants
to hear. She

epicked in the twenties's
wild hours. Said

I sing gossip no
one wants
to hear. She

groaned into market falls
and the depression.

Ain't got no
thing but my life
yall gathered
over there.

Queen of the
dispossessed.
Mother of
night longings.
Keeper of
hard times dues.
Lord, Queen of
the blues.

Remembered

(for Virginia Louise Ferris)

Blues and blues
and blues. I always
remember. I always
surge to rituals
clenched in legacy.
I
can
not run a
way from the world
in a jug. It hangs
back of my mind.
Blues
got the stopper
in its hands.
Blues and blues
and blues. I got.
Blood memory. Ninety
nine years in a breeze.
But take
one hundred for
a wind. The
blues/stopper in
its hands. Whips/

huddled in my ancestors'
legacy. Impulsed
aesthetics. Whips/huddled
in battle array. Impulses
sprinkled
from memory. Blues and
blues and blues
I got. The world
in a jug. My daddy
put it there/with
his aches, ragged memories
ripped by history

The world
in a jug
I got. Blues
got the
stopper in its hands.
I rise each
moment from time
remembered: rituals
blooming space in
side stones. I rise
and rise in
blues and blues.
Time
dripping from seams
in long throats of
dreams. I pour
my day from generations.
On knees of visions.
Forging the word:
the legended prophecy

they kept in brown
eyes/in long midnights of
slave castles. I pour
my night from generations
on backs of dreams.
Forging the word:
hammering longviews
behind moans of adolescent
gods. Hammering worldviews
beneath downcast eyes of
deceit. Hammering homeviews
deep inside hurt. Hammering
the world they kept and
closeted in rhythms.
Time. Clockmusic/they sang
their futures from. Griotmusic
they annotated their past
with.

Howlin Wolf

He
annoints the sun: lingering
spells of its appreciation.
Drag
their tales round night's confined spirit.
Let it
out into urges
only the unfree memorize.
In shacks
and stereotypes covering faces like quilts.
Let it
out into nocturnal transformations
in the bottom.
Where evil going on
flees the superstition of light.
His voice,
a meteor, hurled from distances
in depths of tribulations,
howls willingness in slaves.
They meet
at the cross
roads in memory:
steal three hundred pounds of heavenly joy

from a barrel of footsteps
swimming in muddy pods of dreams.
They march
out of my mind with a whole lotta
lightning in their eyes.
Claim
the darkness as their temple.
Sprinkle
saw
dust over the floor.
Let
the good
times
roll over curses damning
my name.

Bobby Blue Bland

Past the grave. Farther
on up the road of finality.
He reaches from tasselling blood.
My mother had
her youth in and
my grand
mother willed
on Sanders Bottom.
He
reaches and
draws a song
cross night's tongue.
A wordless master
piece defining time.
All
the love blues
didn't steal.
He
gives each
per
for
man
ce with kisses to women

from kitchenettes, kitchens, scrubbing floors
and memories of long rows
and broken men.
Each
ritual he revives preachers
condemned in downcast eyes.
Gives
all the love blues
didn't steal.

Reaches
to touch hands.
Bends
to kiss lips.
Clicks
myths in his throat and
bellows vaults of dust from longings
hardtimes imprisoned.
Opens
gates in his voice and drains
his pain to moods of celebration.
Turns
on the love
light. Lowers
his pain to moods of celebration.
Turns
on the love
light. Changing
folks
like a natural baptism.
Changing evil's face
like a natural healing
lordy, lordy

changing
evil like a healing
found man

Maxwell, May 31, 1987
Old John

I know they call you
Big
Bad
John.

Sold
on a morning.
They play
some
thing hidden.
Some
thing
immersed
in what they own.
In
side secrets.
They hypnotize demons of
jitterbugging ghosts.
Start

blood flowing in dry bones of
exile.
Big
John.
They got
every
thing a nation
needs. Music of
purity. Fresh
and rich. Music
from the gods' voice.
Shango/please
thunder words
on me.
Come/on
Shango, won't
you
please thunder power
on me.
Cause I'm
going to New York
even if I have
to walk. Please
thunder words
on me.

I am blue: Big
John
and the blues
begin in me eyes.
I
grew
up in a cotton boll.

Bred
on a harsh
dry row/crying
rain in August.
Dog
days anchored
their foot
prints
in lean moments
of my growth.
Big
John
I know they call
you
Big
Bad
John but I got
the blues
in
side my mind.

The Blues I See

(for Nancy Ortenberg)

ruts in souls. floods
rising muddy in hearts.
memories cracked/the marrow
imprisoned in diasporic
wanderings. songs bludgeoned
by genocides/ shattered to bits/
hover in my eyes. songs smashed
from tongues of nations:
mandingo, wolof, yoruba,
ashanti, ibo . . . songs crushed
and crushed by tyranny.

journey through midnights.
sounds of desperate owls/hooting
in veins/soon overboard. soon
meshed in anonymity. journey
through silence-bled hours.
where spirits wither from anemia.
journey into perpetual lashes.
long roads and troubles. where
nobody knows your name because
it is changed and changed by
whips. long roads and mothers

and fathers gone; children
orphaned to stillbirths. lovers
with somebody else and debts
falling like hail. long roads
and hope struggling inside a jug;
reaching for windows of day. the
blues I see . . .

Percy Mayfield

From a hot embered speech
reluctant in a witness
tree. Kneeling in cries of
pepper and feathers. The victim
wore in his eyes, round
his head. He loosens
grips of tyranny, slurs me
a river's invitation.
I
went to the river.
It
was a voice crying
in thickets. A big
voice rising from a cotton
sack crying eyes. Shaped
like bolls. Speech was
a witness: Moses Jones
climbs from blue mist
and undulating pitches
of birth. He slow-talked
to idioms of endurance. From
a blues he got in
side ears of molasses.

His momma gave him
on cold mornings of loneliness.
His daddy had only long
gone shadows agitating places
with their doggone hollers.
He took.
This loneliness.
These hollers.
Wrote me a letter
just as long as your right
arm. In
scribed me a river's
invitation. Sealed it
with embered speech.
From a witness tree.
I spoke to the river:
please send me some
one to love.
It spoke back to me.
His voice was the river
and skeletal multitudes
rose from his words.
In blues mists and
moaning my father's name.

Speech

1
They
could tell
it was war.
By
the sound
it made.
If you beat out
memory on its
quivering palms.
People
would know
how to move heads,
twist hips
or legislate feet
by
the sound.
The
drum talked:
Language, history,
myth, ritual,
and memory.
The drum talked

if you planted
rhythms on its skin
and caressed it
with moods of
improvisation

    2
My grand
mother knew not
drums.
Her
pots and
pans talked.
If
she squeezed the dish
rag like wringing
off
a chicken's head and
pondered the depths of
the image
less water
then
the old rooster
was crowing: a storm
was coming.
If
she held the pot
out
like it was a new
born
baby and screened
its rivers of dark flesh
through nets of her vision

then Poppa
was gon die.
Swopping
wings of the angel
was heard
clapping beneath
the grease.
If
she clenched her fist and
shoved it
under water in silence
then
some angel of
mercy was on
its way
to rain
down a little
ease.

If
she rattled pots and
pans like two cats
fussing and fighting
under the house
then
some
body
was messing with her man.
a
low
down
rat

done brought the blues
in
to her happy home.

Echoes

Park Avenue
lies straight a
cross. The portal.
City of New Orleans opened.
Lies near
the left hand of god: where Lefty
Diz
crowns a revival.
Voice
Odom jines in with sermons
Bobby
Bland
folded thirteen
stories
down
in memory of his voice.
Church
he spreads out.
Like goober dust.
Church
he shovels out of
the blue household of
his days.

Church
he initials
on the face of the air.
A
cross a century's heart.
Park
Avenue
lies in riddles.
Lies
stationed from cries.
Legacy
rebounds in echoes.
Language of
Dixie's massacres of spirits.
Assaulted
screams, sounds.
Echoes
from longings and will.
Echoes
pain created
to heal pain.
Dances
with flesh pealing.
Songs of
body moans.
Echoes
the lean deacon of shouts
cries
down through mole holes in bones and
tangled barbed wire of generations.
Cries
a new dimension from ashes of memory.

190

Here as in any place I can
breathe. Talk and I see
with my ears. Follow the
Drinking Gourd of Ancestors:
Elmore, Sonny Boy, Muddy Waters.
Pain and memory/is all I couldn't
lose. I mix'em up to give you
the blues. The small window in
my soul/you can see eternity
through. Here as in any place
I can dream. Talk and I see
with my skin. Neckbones cracking
under weights, flesh melting in
grips of fire, screams injecting
poison in my veins. And I follow
callings in my blue-striped winds
of pain and memory.

197

Over bones
of a moon. Over
owls/witnessing.
Children/wrenched
from childhoods. Led
to plantations under
alien names. Without
songs and sayings and
legends in them. Led
nameless to wicked limbs.
Blood running down
stiffness. Into another
solitary hole. Without
cycles into ancestors.
A black gone. Another
man done gone/they sang.
He led revolts in minds;
stood up, told the boss man
he wasn't gon be cheated
no more. He wasn't gon
see his momma work somebody's
kitchen no more. Wasn't gon
see his daddy cringe before

untruthful judgement scales
no more. Bobo's ghost/rises
every day/in my eyes

201

Earnestine had lemon
nade
        when every
body else
drank
        dust.
Took Robert
from Sista/rode
in
his convertible
for spite.
Every Saturday night/ at Mr. Al's
she swallowed her beer.
Shook
her body. Took
her man＿rode in defiance.
Every Saturday night
she took yestiddies/poured
them in her glass. Drank
without a frown. No
body wanted her to git
evil. Kept her marriage
three decades. Til death.

After
eight children.
                    But she had
ice
water in her
heart

216

Blues/everybody wants
to tell me/is personal
and I nod half-approval.
For I know birth
elevates. I know growth
is sanctity. And adulthood
is divine. For gods/rise
from dreams rolling into
dreams. Everybody gotta
heart. They say/blues
is what everybody feels;
when they connected/ won't let
go hurt. Keep it alive til
they can soothe it to sleep.
Blues/everybody wants to tell
me is a feeling. And I know.
And history. A place be
neath what's seen. And a way
into hearts/back to your own
heart. A sermon of moods/twisted
in sweat and tears. A personal

plea/hitched to a national
agenda. You know/prophecy of a
people.

Groove

1
old niggers
never die.
they
just.
dance hoodoo
on god's schemes.

2
blues. is the floor.
souls congregate. on.
the meeting.
passion. lives will
to rafts.

3
minstrels. with
out stages. blues.
singers. sometimes.
they mimic dreams.
only those
beneath history.

allege to.
know

4

when night hits bones
tongues wing into moods.
as meanings glide
somewhere between whips
and revolt. and we title
the magicians homing songs.
into movement. duke. prez.
and the count of boogies.
head nods and foot pats.
accept.

Billy Branch

I wear the song/behind
the years others forgot.
I play yesterday and sing
tomorrow. My cupped hands
and breathe/talk about me
and you. About dirt roads
and dew. About needing a
woman and being blue. I play
me and I play you. The
goodtimes and the bad. Black
eyes and the best loving
you ever had. About lies
slick folks tell and about
seeing them caught in their
hell. I sing about dreams
that never come true. About
pains and aches too. I wear
the song/behind the years
others forgot. My face is
mischief and halo; I stick
you with my fork and sooth
you with my wings. I am
the boogie man . . .

SOB

True Believers on the road.
Bringing the news. Bearing
our blues. Truebloods on the
road. History in veins of
their riffs, moans, screams.
and boogies. They come from
a hundred midnights of longings.
Bringing the news. Bearing our
blues. From Robert Johnson's
"Sweet Home Chicago"/hellhounds
on their trail. True Believers
on the road. True Bloods. From
John Lee Hooker's beat and slow
rhythms/working sunup to sundown
in cottonfields; the Mississippi
sun and hardships/rising in
his eyes. From Elmo James/ his
pain hurting them too. Bringing
the new. Bearing our blues.
They hoboed "Smokestack Lightning"
with Howlin Wolf/getting on the
pony of naked winds. Bucking way
up in the middle/of Sunnyland palms

of a harmonica playing sky. Bearing
our blues. From Lucille's /slim
strings of wonder/menchildren
of tomorrow. Bringing the news.
Sons of blues. Bearing our news.
Sons of blues. Sons of blues.

Instrument

(from Rosa's Lounge)

Muddy Waters/looks
out/through leaves of
smoke. A guitar sends
dewdrops to messages.
The night refuses to tell.
The private wars
Mississippi scarred
in eyes. Night refuses
to tell. A guitar in
forms a decalogue of
terror. The weight and
depth of downcast visions.
A guitar tutors eyes as
Muddy Waters pours
out of cotton/sacks and
distances in/side weeping
hearts. Time resides in
tunnels. The guitar
excavates from Ogun/squatting
in a weight
lifter's
posture. To heave history.
His

voice
walks a mojo plank
to summons. Shouts/to
revive words drowned
in cups of rhythms.
Loas carved on hands of
spirits. Who dripped
pieces of
skin from wing
tips. Blues shop
lift lost tones from Muddy
Waters/as a guitar in
forms tomorrows

Long
shadows, long tongues:
the blues.
The blues.
Windows in muddy
legends/rise to
construct temples. I
live my mother's and
my father's birth in.
Poems
I peel from rinds.
Colors of talk. My
grandfather prayed
to poor land. Colors of
silence. The time/folks
spent living be
hind bricks. The Majority
piled over. What
they could

not see in
side them
selves. Colors of
swaying hips and
laughter in hands.
Colors of
the shouts they ringed a
round jubilee eyes.
Colors of
memory: secrets of
baptism and calling
on the Lord's
legions. Calling
long and
deep
on subtle waves
in veins. Colors of
quick deaths. Cries
and contortions in
speech.

Colors of
the place god
put his voice. The
harmonica moaning.
Rivers of
conversation. Metal
prophecies crying
echoes in cupped
hands of legacy.
Metal
seances. Blues/the
closest thing

to talk
in
g to god.
Metal
cravings of dreams.
Exposed
in palms and breath.
Colors of
music: thin mists of
pain
raining
down. Night on
its knees/praying
for a song.

Maxwell Sunday

Opening lines
of sorrow. Lurrie
Bell recites/with
laughter. A son
of history. What gave
my grand
daddy his humped back.
He recites. Legends.
Tales of
my grand
mother's years toiling.
He recites.
Blues. Out
side his temple.
A son
of blues. Raining
down his dues in smiles.
The life my parents
never knew/buried be
hind Dixie and leaves
of time. He recites.
Rhythms in
his eyes. Rivers

of blues. Out
side his shrine. A
wanderer/wayfaring
backstreets and crying.
A
bout to camp be
tween the
gaps in some brother's
teeth. He kneels
down in ancestry
and memory/hollers
a delta/early in
a mother-in-law's
hand/waving
good
bye and bye.
He recites obituaries
of lost hours/interred in
side a black skin. Dances
a crib of moans.

A son/nightfarer of
time. Who
out
distances foot
prints spirits
retrench to/in
bellies of
memory. Bellies of
the morning his daddy
fled Dixie for these
crowded/lonely hours
where he rises from

darkness and plays
so well/my history
he is able to
tell. . . .

Blues for Leon Forrest

I got the blues of a fallen
teardrop. Prostrate on the mercy
bosom/pushed down, way down/a long
ways from home of the spirit. Way
back home/ in a corner where big foots
of indifference/steps on my patented
leather hopes. Deep down near
wayfaring roots and Lucifer socked
conspiracy in scars of wayside dwelling
children/living in the Bucket of Blood
of despair. I got the real/unbaptized
blues. Bone dust of lost souls blues.
I got the Invisible Man cellar blues.
That's why I be so bad I hire
a metaphysical wheelbarrow to haul
my scrambled soul around. Got the bone
dust blues/testified before a sky.
Dripping with blood of my folks.
The fallen teardrop blues. Water
rinsed red in polluted eyelids
of clouds/acid alienness of hate

and oppression. The apocalypse blues
of falling eyewater/drifting down
unabridged cracks in concern. Falling
slowly down blues. The soundless
disappearances of dreams in a teardrop.
I got the blues/a long ways from Satchmo
and the mask of my humanity. I got
the long ways from home blues/got
the fallen teardrop blues

Burning Up in the Wind

Got a little story I like to tell
when that sweet thing done left you
when your nerve soother done gone
and you talk about it, can't help yourself

I'm twisting, turning, lifted higher and higher
I'm twisting, turning, lifted higher and higher
Whoever said you need a plane to fly, sure is a liar

Because I am tossed, turned, and all belted down
Because I am tossed, turned, and all belted down
When I look I am ninety miles above the ground

My easy roller done gone and I got the begging sin
My easy roller done gone and I got the begging sin
All hot and sweating cause I'm burning up in the wind

If you got a good thing, don't ever live a lie
If you got a good thing, don't ever live a lie
Cause you might end up hanging from a cross of fire

Like a lynchee, Lord, flames reaching for my face
Like a lynchee, Lord, flames reaching for my face
My baby's gone and there just ain't no hiding place

My easy roller done gone and I got the begging sin
My easy roller done gone and I got the begging sin
All hot and sweating cause I'm burning up in the wind

Callings

(for Charlie Braxton)

O dark winged hawk zooming down on eyes
O blues
O remembrances
O silhouetted predator swooping down
O blues
O remembrances
O lice sticking inside my mind
O blues
O remembrances
O plastic adobe windows shut tight
O blues
O remembrances
O folks can dream but not in my sleep
O blues
O remembrances
O mystic gorer of ages scarring perceptions
O blues
O remembrances

O sounds of vines in hearts
O men tugging memory home
O Mississippi shouters
O delta wise/men in over/alls

O field hands harvesting tales
O singers of doom
O plenty good room in laughter
O night eyes of dungeon tales
O wandering pain mongers of joy
O men in debt with wealth in their voices
O prophets of life denied pulpits
O unknown memories of generations
O songs of being
O songs of essence
O songs of life
O singers of life before God turned his back
O songs of life
O music of my blood spilled in sacrifices of
   love
O music of my heritage planted in a nation's
   ears
O blues

O remembrances
O home/land interpretations
O discarded treasures vaulted in stubborn
   troubadours
O hanged dreams cutting the rug from limbs
O remembrances
O insinuated mountains caught in a moan
O doom-sayed eyes with Anansi's gifts
O blues singers
O music of cellar-lored steps to eternity
O blues
O remembrances
O farther on up the road
O spirits dancing in circles

O winged tongues breaking earth
O grave/breaking tongues
O silence/defying voices
O blues
O remembrances
O groove sharpening pits of fire
O masks of rebirth painted red
O the night time/is the right time seasons
O slow dragging steps of whips
O blues

O separation
O folks can steal my blues
O but they didn't pay my dues
O they took me to the burying place
O the blues put life back into my face
O redeeming pathos of woe
O time bleeding across worlds
O blues/how I love you so
O songs
O life sifted through pain
O good/times pulled from the devil's jaws
O blues
O remembrances
O cotton/fields of strangulation
O scaled accomplices of greed
O cotton gins
O let me tell you how the blues be/gin
O separation
O long journeys through terror
O wide river spitting out sand
O Mississippi
O life behind shadows of God's back

O hell bitten land if you are black
O blues
O remembrances
O shacks frightened of winds
O the long roads to self
O down/cast eyes
O subservient actions
O peace coming when the wind cries

O it's in the news
O it's in the news
O blues
O remembrances
O singer
O legended arranger of tales
O shaper of lore
O blues man
O blues
O remembrances
O little red rooster
O spoon/full
O I'm ready
O wang dang doodle
O muscle man of songs
O foundation builder of values
O griot
O back door man
O blues
O remembrances
O I ain't superstitious
O do the do
O you shook me
O they took his blues to rock

O they put his blues in pop
O I just wanna make love to you
O blues heaven angel of dreams
O black bard telling it straight
O blues father of the city
O Mississippi wanderer spreading life
O griot
O blues singer
O it don't make sense (you can't make peace)
O it's in the news
O it's in the news
O you don't make sense
O you don't make sense
O when you can't make peace
O blues
O blues

O he stood up from Harvard
O he answered in Greek and Latin
O he was illiterate
O they asked him what Chinese symbols on
    laundry meant
O he said, "That they don't want me to vote."
O blues
O remembrances
O they told her Constitution Hall could not be
    used
O the nation cried out in shame
O she sang and tears poured from her heart
O blues
O remembrances
O color curtains
O backseats

O tears remembering those never making it
O blues
O remembrances
O songs

O Green Pastures
O remember "de Lawd"
O how he was received by the Texas Governor
O when he boarded the train
O remember/conductor said, "Nigger, you
    can't ride in no Pullman"
O remember "de Lawd"
O blues
O remembrances
O when I wanted to smoke
O I asked for Prince Albert
O they showed me the picture on the can
O they said, "Say, Mister Prince Albert"
O blues
O remembrances
O long time coming dreams
O hopes crushed under heels

O do you know about the blues
O are you illiterate in back/handed good news
O I don't believe you know the blues
O I kinda think you ain't been down and out
O don't think you been where they brung it
    home at
O don't believe you can use any down/home
    blues
O don't believe you don't know no/thing about
    dues

O do you know the blues
O don't believe you know my blood cradled
    aches
O don't know if you know a womb threatened
    melody
O don't know if you got any clues
O blues
O remembrances
O some folks get a globe to tell where blues
    be/gin
O do you know the crimes whips committed
    against my skin
O blues
O remembrances
O know the blues from grooves cut across my
    back
O know the reason cause I born black
O blues
O remembrances

O blues
O remembrances
O my time cast in chains
O dreams in/side coffins
O blood running like water/falls
O land of difficult hearing
O Medgar falling in creations
O passing the hat
O NAACP
O women for struggle
O black black
O life after shadows died
O life after blood

O ever/green laughter in eyes
O black women bending
O mothers doing and doing
O dark night hounds on trails
O fathers talked about
O blues
O remembrances
O land of doors shut in my face
O whips giving me my sense of place
O they may wander in/to my shack
O but they won't take my story back
O blues
O remembrances

O generations knowing stunted heavens
O worshipping people of faith
O back/logs of a nation's culture
O Africans
O conjuring messengers of immortality
O unmarked graves
O no/body knows my joy
O no/body knows my heart's voice
O my nose is in the sand
O the blues is where I stand
O language of eternity
O language of pulsing blood
O language of silence
O language of anguish
O language of weeping
O language of stubbornness
O language of improvisation
O I don't need a translator for my pain
O it keeps falling, hurrying down like rain

O blues
O remembrances

O unknown hands lining my soul
O voices listening to hopes
O bellows
O screams
O moans
O shouts
O hollers
O groans
O birth place of songs
O miles and miles of cotton
O time when humanity is for/gotten
O voices listening to re/birth
O chanters of forbidden riddles
O toilers in dirt
O thrivers in spirits
O ancestors enduring much hurt
O women of neglect
O women of history
O women of fear
O women of hard work
O women of prayer
O women of courage
O women making a way
O women of generations
O women of wisdom
O birth place of songs
O blues
O remembrances

O people with/out history
O people telling it all
O worried minds of America
O people cramped under chains
O people way/faring alien paths
O wanderers from town to town
O people denied inns at home
O people al/ways having to roam
O temperament of strugglers
O never turned back moaners at day/break
O troubles troubles al/ways coming
O crimes against skin passing
O Medgar
O Fannie Lou prophetess of needs
O unknown martyrs of progress
O keep on going people of promise
O tales untold in history books
O hurt kept legacy
O despised legacy of truth
O legacy dipped in muddy tears
O Mississippi memories kept
O songs where gods have wept
O blues
O remembrances

O geography manned with terror
O home/land of pain and joy
O place with a hiding place
O I'm gonna bring it on home
O land where the haints roam
O geography of blood
O place of a perpetual flood

O stalks of injustice a/long side roads
O harvest of dusty tears raining on wills
O geography manned with neglect
O heels of America trampling dreams
O the sky is crying
O every/time I get a woman/Tin Pan Alley
   take her way from me
O it nine below zero/and she put me out for
   another man
O blues
O remembrances
O I'm going down down
O I'm gonna bring it on home
O long memory of the silent man
O long memory of unmarked graves
O tortured memory of slaves
O I'm gonna bring it on home
O every/time I start testifying
O I look down/and even the page is crying

Billie Holiday

(for Dottie Abbott)

Feel and hear.
Her insistence on in
side lore. Personal in
jury. Subpoenaed
by tears dripping in silence.
After each throb
has surrendered.
To epochs of stillness.
She
rises from impulses of
hurt/to sing fine
print on the pain.
Employs
a microscope in her ears.
Crawls a
round in silence.
Finds
diurnal slaps side TJ's head.
Immersed
in his knocks on
her back. Feels deep,
his screams stick in
her fingers. After

digging/she hears
Lottie Jean's mis
carriages groan
in her lungs. She
hums history
when she opens
her mouth
in silence.
Her night
quilts stories from depths
in her touches
I can
not let
go and I
can
not keep the music.
She feels and I
hear deep with
in flesh of tones.
I
believe/I'll
go back
to college and
major in kneeling
with my ears.

Big Mama Thornton

(sang original version of "Hound Dog")

Barking.
Just a barking
up.
Sleeves of a vine.
Treeing
rain from tabloids of shade.
She
beats the hound
dog with rhythms.
Sends
indebted pleas of her church
up
through barks. Climbing sleeves.
Messes a
round tongues. Planting
roots in speech.
Messes a
round chaos/setting limits
out in my eyes.
Barking.
Just a barking

up.
Sleeves of a vine.
Solitary. Clinging
to a limb of
hope.
My
grand
father left my will in.

She
throws a howl
up
through a hound
dog.
Barking.
Just a barking
and it multiplies limbs.
For vines.
She
exists: barking.
Just a barking
up
sleeves of survival.
And I climb
down
from my name
screamed on pages of leaves.
Crying
her lasting sense of
speech.

Koko Taylor

She
holds her mojo out
to a bar.
Tender. Who.
Was my father.
Who was my mother's brother.
Was my longings.
Puts a
wang
dang
doodle loop
round retired dreams.
Pitches a
cannon
ball on toes of
stillness.
Calls
apron-wearing nannies
back from big houses.
Calls
uncle-toming butlers
from pockets of myth.
Holds

her mojo out
to a bar.
Tender. Who.
Was celebration.
All
night/long.
All
night/long.
Puts
great specks of time
on folks. And they
slay stillness.
Follow
a wang
dang
doodle loop.
All
night/long.
All
night/long.

Big Maybelle

(for Angela Jackson)

She
parks her sorrows
near a curb, gets
out of
her skin and
stumbles
up steps of pleas.
Un
listening, at
tentative and calloused
hearts
tune
in.
She
gets back in
her skin, cries off
down the long boulevard of
memory.
Her pain in
her voice/her
people's in
her veins.

Under Class

(for Wardell and Katie Mae)

There are
dreams in dreams. A
landscape of labyrinths.
Bessie Smith
held backwater inside
her pleas
of broken dreams.
She
held the middle passage
in her moans
and brought good news
to another day.
Another
dream to live. And
nightmares are dreams
abused.
Catacombs of bruised
words/resurrected.

She is sixteen, pregnant.
A day
after her 17th birth

day/a baby.
A dream bruised
in Cutter's absence
and the long rows ahead.
Her heritage/burning
rags and descent
into blues. The pine
topped vision of women
answerable to hills
on redclay. Their spirits
making green
to grow in pain.
She is nineteen;
a second son is
her 20th birth
day gift. 1940 in war
and mistreating clods
to hoe.

The dream lies
down mighty low in turmoil
of weeds. Rots
with maggots stealing
promises from youth.
Hearts/ punctured
by absences. Dreams
bruised into generations.
A chronology
of blues. Trips
from Saunders Bottom
to rheumatism in her mother's
joints/break the dream.
Bedridden/with yesterday

pulling her dreams
into its night.

She
has Bessie Smith's pig
foot and empty bed
in dreams. The men/
left behind screens
of soot reside in halos
of swinging ropes.
Nineteen
years old/got ways
just like a baby child.
There are dreams
in dreams. Bessie Smith
sang her through
her grandma's troubles/
down to her footprints
on dreams/she never saw.
Ask her
where you going/and she
tell you where she been.
There are dreams
in dreams. Two sons
two fathers. Nineteen
years old. Ask her
where you going/ and she
tell you where she been.
Then she
start a conversation
that ain't never got
an end. Girlhood and
womanhood come/same time.

Men/gone like shadows
at noon. Into the next
bruised dreams.

Robert Johnson
got the men standing
at the crossroads.
Their heads
hung down and crying
parched moans of dawn.
The men/images of
possibility, stand
against the weather.
They mold
their dreams after foot
prints their fathers
got whipped into.
Images of cotton
and a troop of boll weevils.
Bruised
dreams. The men/left her.
With two sons and
withered behind quarters
and places where debts
swallow tomorrows.
There are dreams
in dreams. The men
separate from her and
wander in shadows, longing
"Sweet Home Chicago."
But vines of redclay
hills yank their dreams
back to bottomlands and

long rows and a wide
river of sorrow. They
go to Church/Sunday morning,
Lord knows,
they fall on their knees.
Pray so long/even the devil
hears their pleas.

Every
Sunday morning
They
fall down on
their knees/fall down
on their pleas.
Swap
their blues rising
in their eyes
for testifying.
Every
thing their daddies
got whipped for/they
beg and stomp eye
sight from Sonny Boy's
hands. Get help
from echoes/his black name
ringing all up/and down
eternity. They
be stilled in blues
in their prayers/wavering
in air. Touching
nerves of walls.
Motionless, they call
and call Muddy Waters

from a Mojo Hand with
the honeychild/swamp water
incensing his tales
of fire. His blues
and nothing to lose.
Get help
from Elmo James/talking
to his baby on the telephone
of trill guitar tremors.
His blues and
nothing to lose

Nine
teen years old:
the dream
died, resurrected
in shouts never
heard. Licks
from fields plaster
blisters on eyes.
Dreams age
into next stalk
knocking seasons.
They
stare at uprooted futility
and expanding territory.
Die
in mud beneath a pine
redclay on a hill.
Nineteen
years old. The wick
is jerked from skies;
a dark mist of ashes covers shades

of rising days. Nine
teen years old and
trouble, troubles
seem/to always follow
her around. All those
years/the dream moving
in her like a baby and
never able to be held.
Stillbirth.
Bruised dreams
aging.

She
cried out/in
testimony but couldn't
hear
her own
voice. She
was in a
song and the song
was blues.
She
was sung into wakefulness
and could feel earth
quakes of sound
rumbling in a dark
cavern. Laughter
nearly ejected her
to daylight but silence
locked her inside
the song again. Nine
teen years old.
They breathed her

down, belched her
toward light.
She
was a blues song;
the past
was every day.
They
sung her, cried her
screamed
her, shouted her, and
howled her. Nine
teen years old: two
sons, two fathers,
no man. She was
a blues song.

The men.
Who left her.
Had
their blues
and nothing to lose.
Stayed out/
a century chasing
a dream: in
bottles, Georgia
Skin, dice, and
a dream with
nothing to lose.
They
left her with the
blues they got
from their day's
rot.

Men
of game chasing
a dream into dreams.
They
headed north for
a dream. Rinsed
dust from ears
for a dream. Wore
starched shirts
and polished shoes
for a dream. They are
played all the time:
picked by cotton sack
fingers, squeezed with
palms of longing and
slid over with cupped
hands of supplication.

They
heard her: nine
teen years old.
From way
down and they
hollered but fingers
slid over their attempts,
drowning out
their calls.
She
was in the voice
and they inside
the guitars. They
were a blues song;
it birthed them and

nurtured them. They
were moving. Canton.
Had
their blues and
nothing to lose.
The men
tried to call her
again, but were slid
over, picked
and squeezed.
Then blown out
and sucked
back in. As her
broken promises
talked to them.
Mendenhall. And their
skinned cries of
longing reached but she
was too far
down below/way inside
the voice. Under
the moans. They couldn't
communicate
because they were
a blues song.
Grenada.

The men's
minds read letters
from dreams
they chased:
up north,
you go

when you wanna
go, where you wanna
go,
work, git paid
every Friday,
dress up,
drive your big
car out to party.
Up north, got lights, toilets
inside and you talk
back and fight back
when somebody
mess with you.
Work here if you
willing to work.
Up north,
houses don't shake
when storms come and
wells and cisterns
don't run dry.
Up north
you kin git you
something and be
on your own. Folks
is just folks.
That color stuff
don't exist.
Batesville.

The letters
she yelled
didn't tell. The
history. They

reached for
her/but the voice
whiskeyed and longing
drew her
in its pulses and
bellowed ten miles
of hurt
over her initiatives.
Long
time she cried
to developing triumphs
of fingers/sliding gates
of moods over the men.
Long
time
inside the voice talking
about its baby or
on some back
street crying/she
struggled to be.

Memphis.
The fingers push
the men farther
in Lucille's teeming memory.
Nine
teen years old.
They
lose Howlin Wolf at the bottom
with the woman they left
calling
from Smokestack Lightening.
Lucille

holds them in her squeals
and trembling
admittances of pain.
Nine
teen years old.
They
take their soul from brown
paper bags and
hobo out on Lucille's
midnight wanderings.
Hitting
the road of dreams,
going
up north. Dyersberg.
The faint
echoes of her softness
revives yesterday. Sweet
sixteen/just left her home
and the sweetest
thing they ever seen.
Then she
was nineteen years
old/ways just like a baby
child. They left her
and all she got/is the blues
they gave her.

Chasing
dreams with their
blues. The men
leave nights of their
legends: I said,
git up ol' black,

and would please
move over, mister
gray.
They
chase a place
their children
may work
with pencils behind
their ears.
Fulton.
The men
go from a place
for a dream. The
Mississippi blues
imprison them
in rusty strings.
And they squirm,
kick, and yell
for a voice; for
the pain they gave
her. Their blues
rub salt
into their eyes
and they cry resurrection.
But the
blues song
holds them
in anonymity of
crying. Cairo,

All/the love
they gave her/the
blues took away.

Nine
teen years old.
They
left her for a dream.
1940s and
dreams bloomed
like sun
flowers. She clutched
the hand
that was shook.
As the voice
talked a blues
book.
No
body heard her steps
in Big Momma Thornton's hound
dog/just barking
at dreams.
She
straddled the tongue,
peered, hoping
to see the
men. But fingers
plowed over
them, choked
screams from long tales
of untold
blues/the whip gave
in magnolia breezes.
They were
born in the blues, lived in
the blues, died
in the blues. They

were a blues song.
Effingham.

The blues
begin
in a story with
out an end.
The real
passion
of time. Nineteen
years old.
A world
of dry moss;
dreaming cracking
like parched earth.
A world/empty
of possession.
Men/chasing
dreams. 63rd Street.
Their
blues and nothing
to lose.
Shadows
they run from
got the
blues they know.
Bruised
dreams and memory
of debts, hard
clods, and death.
Mississippi,
Mississippi blues
they leave.

Ain't got nothing
but bad memories
clutching at a sleeve.
Bruised
dreams and the
dream they chase.
12th Street Station;
final stop.

The men fall out/on fossils
of dreams.
Tenements
frozen in time.
The blues
they had/gone.
They
no longer could hear
the woman
they left.
Nine
teen years old:
two sons,
two fathers.
They were the
blues but
their song
was gone.
The voice
of memory
in her loneliness.
The guitars pawned
to credit lines.
She

disappears in silence,
falls side
memory of the love
they gave her:
two sons,
two fathers.
Nine
teen years old.

Chicago
blues/got them
humping/for
dreams. With
nothing to lose.
They
in rhythms of
work; inside
each move
ment of the clock.
And
the blues
they left
her. Crushed
by bricks and
pavement. Chicago
got them
and their memory.
Chicago blues,
Chicago blues,
got them paying
working dues.
They
long the guitars

and fingers
shouting life.
Long
her voice
from beneath moans.
But
they fell out/
on fossils and
Chicago blues
grabbed
their collars.

Nine
teen
years old; she
gave birth
to her fourth
child. Different
daddies for
each. Some
where running
wild. Chicago
blues/stock
yards and canning
jobs they
lose.
Stock
yards and canning jobs
gone/a little
man
hood they lose.
Stock
yards and canning jobs

gone.
Men/without work
hungry
dogs without a bone.
Mean
and they fight
til they sleep.
Jobs gone
left them wearing
empty bellies and
all alone.

She is thirteen,
pregnant.
And he left
her after that
day. he was
thirty and had her
at his sister's
house. All the
love he /said
he had /he gave her
with a full belly.
Now
she is fourteen,
pregnant.
He is a drop
out
eighth grader.
Who loved
her. Gave her
the blues/some
body left at the station

when they fell out
on fossils. Gave
her a baby
and pain. Bruised
dreams and memory.

Then
she is six
teen years old: the
sweetest thing I
ever seen.
Just left her home,
pregnant.
Stock
yards and canning
jobs gone. The
men/left her
with the blues
they gave her.
Bruised
dreams. They hit
her, punch her in
the stomach.
She
is nine
teen years old: about
to have her fourth
child. And they hit
her in the stomach,
step on her with twisting
heels, bounce up and
down

on her from leaps.
She screams out
to history but realizes
she is
the drum and a
blues song is
being played. She
is the dance
floor and a ritual
is taking place.

The men
who left her/she
hears from in
side lyrics/they
drowning in music
and cannot hear.
They/a blues
song/and she
the drum.
Nine
teen years old; about
to have her fourth child.
The men
leap
up
from suctioning of
grinding tongues.
But slurred accusations
of speech dip them
into generations of the

blues they gave her.
And they drown
in music.

He is four
teen/aiming at a twelve
year old; a baby
child, Lord,
killing a baby. He
shoots
his shot and shadow
of a pre-teen falls
into headlines: with
the blues and nothing
to lose. He is six
teen/aiming at a seven
teen year old; a baby
child killing
a baby.
They
are sentenced to listening;
hear loud reports
screaming from skin
of night. The strange
noise they in; cry
them, holler.
them, shout them, hit
them, shake them, kick
them, and start going
down
down.
Drowning in
the music.

They heard the blues they gave
her/pleading from bloody
leaves of the wind

Nine
teen years old.

Their blues
on its knees
pleading from bloody
leaves of the sind.

Nine
teen years
old;
she/about to have
her fourth child.

Nine
teen years old;
the men/with
out jobs/running a
round like some
body wild.

Chicago blues,
Chicago blues
got them paying
history's dues

Ask them/where
they going
they tell you
where they been.

Nine
teen years old;
the gitting off
the train blues
they got. The lost
culture blues they
got.

Chicago blues,
Chicago blues,
got them paying
history's dues.

Nine
teen years old; they
start a conversation
that ain't never
got an end.

Nothing
I kin do
to please them/get
these young folks
satisfied.

Chicago blues,
Chicago blues,
got them paying
history's dues.

Wind

(for Daniel Clardy)

The blues walks in slow/
dancing.
A woman holds her man's
pain in her steps.
The man
closets his concern in
sacred masculinity.
Lifts
his fist. To mask
all
the love he can
not admit.
The music
walks in/yesterday's
speech. Rolls timbres of
affirmation. Years done
pushed
down with images.
The old
country walking
and talking back
woods clod
hopper. No teeth,

big
feet and colors/loud
enough to challenge
an A-bomb. Telling
his troubles. His
woman/tallow perfuming
her hair. Rips
the proverbial head
rag from her spirit/stands
prophetic: with her pride
waving in air like corn
silk.
The
blues takes this story/puts
it
in the face of immortality.
Shakes
its head/lets
its ancestral bone
slip. Tacks declarations
on confinement.
Mates
its words over the bonding pond of
drought.
And the music/rolls.
Rolls.
Rolls.

Heartbeat

Blues/picks
up my time.
Changes it in
to thunder clapping
pews of sky. The Reverend
Hail Storm, a jack
leg preacher. Sits
by his side.
On the left,
near
the barrel of moans and
groans/he soaking. Blues
bends a hand full of air
til it screams, then
he chunks it in
with the moans and groans.
Jostles
my time up and down in
to the boiling pot of blood.
Draws
a grin over his face
and spits my time
back to memory.

And I write
transformations. Changes
the blues
stitched in my tie.
And I
cry through my pen
til pulses of the page be
come regular

Robert Johnson

Crawls shouts and cracks
in my memory.
Spits
seeds/short breaths of
ecstasy's faith.
Comes in
twined
with soot and gravel.
His walking shoes
tore down/all
most level with my mind.
Blues
all a
around his head.
He got
the slow/walking
blues: five hundred miles
done wore out
his shoes.
Criss
crosses moods in my tones.

Feasts
on worries my grand

father prayed nightly.
Crunches
on the penitentiary of my for
got
ten miles of/feelings.
and I
wake
up mumbling at the cross
roads/my head
hung
down and I. Crying
poison/whips
hissed-screamed
in my past. And
the windows/painted
with blood in my soul
crack. As he shouts
my future in a half
cry/half
late evening moon
and I.
Crawl a thousand
steps/for his voice.
Hell
hounds on my trail
Hell
hounds on my trail.

Rebirth

Like
the moon. Blues
singers rise
from
Tin
Pan
Alleys. Trash and
bar
be
cue grease/embraced
in one
hundred
ten de
gris gris in
the shade.
Words crawl
on their knees,
reach
lids of John
Henry's
boasts and
every
thing gon

be
all right. In the
Full Nelson/tones
exchange with
rhythm
jokes on wishes.
Liquid
transcendence
drips from Billy's
hands.
Blues
singers/come
out
each history. Music
music
and music. Day be
gins its journey.
Time sees
my open aching
worries. I call
from ditches of
my neighbor's
days

Yoknapatawpha

(for Sister Thea Bowman)

Ghosts.
Live out there some
where ben
eat
h a county of
mud.
The
old black man
I
saw
in
the mirror.
Resides
on a tenant plot.
My name
scrawled
on
the open grave.
With visions
Meredith over
came. With visions
Fannie
Lou/rinsed in her starched

tones of Sojourner.
The
old black man,
my fathers's
father.
Lives
in this county
beneath mud.

Official

(for William Faulkner)

1
You
get your stamp.
Folks
pack in to
buy the honor.
But not
your words.

2
They
can
not honor
a living witness.
The pen
would
get too up
pity. Claim blood
stains.
As signs.
Wanna
circulate among truths
nailed down.

3

Dilsey
does
not make the occasion.
Though she
sent tales from yesterday's
letters.
She
mailed with fidelity:
with a tattered
thumb to in
form all:
your black
folks/exist in your novels.
Hers
rake leaves and
pick up paper a
cross hallowed lyceums.
Where Meredith
wrote a chapter
with his spirit and

There
are no sanctuaries
here/for
memory

Saturday Night Decades

(for Langston Hughes, Originator)

I dug your bull
dozing a
round in my weariness.
Your fingers
tickling lead
belly keys in doom.
To pry
the New Negro
from plantations.
I
got my first season
inked by hurt Simple's feet
moaned
over tenderness of
my river of longings.
Hey now:
daddy
young griot of dawn.
Hip
linguist of Harlem
Diaspora. With centuries

bleeding culture
from your tongue.
Sundiata of Harlem,
shoving a porch of opening
from stereotypes.
Hey now:
quilter of folk
lored patches/black
folk stitched from spirits.
Singer of steps I must
take on nameless streets
in my lonely hours.

Hey now:
sundiata of Harlem,
Original legender of my time.

Hey now:

Beginning

My story does
not have
an end. In
side the story in
side my parents.
I got it/from in
a monkey's shadow.
Signifying
eyes. Cried
its secrets/in
to tone puddles of lines.
I pour down on daggers
the page welcomes me
with